Denise Oldenberg Marks, M.D.

THE WORLD THAT WAS BEFORE ADAM!

THE WORLD THAT WAS BEFORE ADAM!

Copyright © 2015

By

Denise Sharbono Marks, M.D.

ISBN-13: 978-1519476388
ISBN-10: 1519476388

Published in Mountain Home, Arkansas by Denise Sharbono Marks, M.D.

The author and publisher, Denise Sharbono Marks, M.D. is a physician who practiced medicine in rural Arkansas between 1988-2010. She was the owner of the Rural Medical Clinic in Dover, Salem, Horseshoe Bend and Witt Springs, Arkansas. She is currently involved in writing articles and books related to nutrition, natural health treatments and cures as well as weight loss. Being a former Marine and serving during the Vietnam era, she is also interested in working with veterans who have PTSD.   She is also a former biology, chemistry, physics, and health and physical education teacher.

This book is dedicated to her two sons, Jason and Justin Sharbono and their families as well as her foster boys, but especially to Jessie who is one of her foster sons that was fascinated about dinosaurs and prehistoric life and fossils.

THE WORLD THAT WAS BEFORE ADAM

I would like to present a plausible explanation as to why planet earth and its prehistoric life forms may be possibly millions of years old and yet present life forms, of which man is the last and highest of God's creation, are very young-probably 6,000 years young. **(Note, the Jewish New Year celebration, Rosh Hashanah 2015, recognizes the Lord God created Adam and Eve 5,776 years ago.)**

The concept of Lucifer and the fallen angels existing on planet earth, possibly millions of years before Adam and Eve were created, has not been expounded upon by scientific writers and only by a few religious writers.

The Bible, more specifically **Revelations 12:7-9**, tells of a time when there was a war in Heaven. This war was between the godly angels, led by Michael, and the demon-like angels, led by Lucifer. This war ended with Lucifer and his band of angels being thrown out of Heaven. They possibly descended to planet earth during the Mesozoic era. It is interesting to note that scientific writers illustrate this era as being very beautiful and fruitful and full of pre-historic life, viz., dinosaurs. The fossil record reveals that huge numbers of beautiful and fascinating plants and amazingly huge creatures existed during the Mesozoic era.

Prehistoric earth (before any written record of historic events by humans such as Adam and Eve) was probably encircled by an ozone-like layer and possibly a water vapor layer. The effect of both of these layers and other atmospheric layers would have produced a green house effect. This in turn, would have supported the abundant prehistoric life that existed during the Mesozoic Era. Many scientists believe this era existed millions of years ago and lasted for millions of years.

The inspired Biblical writer of Genesis 2:4-5 indicates the Lord God created prehistoric earth in separate stages (eras). The King James version of **Genesis 2:4-5** states; "*these are the generations (ages) of the heavens and of the earth when they were created, in the day that the Lord God made the earth and the heavens, and every plant of the field before it was in the earth and every herb of the field before it grew; for the Lord god had not caused it to rain upon the earth and there was not a man to till the ground*".

The Hebrew Bible also indicates that "*the earth that was before the earth that is*" (planet earth) was created beautiful. **Isaiah 45:18** implies God's original creation was not created "tohou" (viz., empty, void, desolate). "Tohou", in Hebrew, means empty, void, desolate and/or without form. This verse in English then - means; "Lord God did not create planet earth empty void or desolate and without form. In fact, both **Isaiah 45:18 and Jeremiah 4:23:27** indicate that the original planet earth was created beautiful and fruitful.

God's Word also indicates in **Isaiah 14:12-17** that Lucifer was planning to ascend back into Heaven and take over God's throne. **This was a rebellious scheme, (orchestrated by Lucifer), to usurp God's authority.** The Bible indicates that this rebellious scheme of Lucifer is the reason God destroyed prehistoric planet earth. These scriptures also indicate that God did not completely destroy or make a full end of planet earth at that time. However, this catastrophic destruction would probably have destroyed all life as we know it, even the demon like forms of Lucifer's fallen angels. This prehistoric life, including demons, actually became fossilized. The fat like substance of this prehistoric life, viz., dinosaurs, saber tooth tigers, mammoths, etc. probably became the source of today's oil and gas resources.

Many scientists believe a catastrophic event did take place at the end of the Mesozoic Era. They theorize that the mysterious disappearance of prehistoric life was caused by severe climate changes. One theory is that a giant meteor hit earth and exploded. Another theory is that there was an increase in volcanic and earthquake activity during this era. Either or both of these theories would have produced a world-wide dust cloud. As a result of either of these catastrophic events, the sun's light and thermal heat would have been blocked.

Note; without the sun's light rays and thermal heat - all life would die. Also, planet earth could have been literally turned upside down - as revealed by many of the land formations we presently see all around us

The Bible also indicates there was a lapse in time between God's original creation of planet earth and the partial destruction of earth's surface and the "re-creation" of the present atmosphere, landscape and life forms. Many religious scholars and writers refer to this lapse in time as "**The Gap Theory of Creation**". This lapse in time may have been thousands or millions of years. Scriptural evidence of the "Gap Theory" can be found in **Isaiah 45:18, Isaiah 14:12-17, Revelations 12:7-9, Jeremiah 4:23-27, Genesis 1:1-29, Genesis 2:4-5 and 2nd Peter 3:5-7**.

The Bible is the first written record of earth's history. There is no written evidence anywhere that man existed before Adam and Eve. The Lord God inspired the original writers of the Hebrew and Greek Bible books and gave them knowledge not only about revelation and prophecy, but also, the Lord God gave these inspired writers knowledge about prehistoric events on planet earth.

The "Gap Theory of Creation" is more clearly understood when we use the words found in the original manuscripts of the Hebrew and Greek books of the Bible. For example, in Hebrew, the word for "was" is "hayah" and "hayah" means; "became"; the Hebrew word for "wilderness" is "tohou" and "tohou" means;"empty, void, without form, desolate or in a state of confusion"; and the Hebrew word for "moved" is "rachaph" and "rachaph" means; "in deep thought".

With these definitions in mind it is easier to understand the following scriptures. In **Isaiah 45:18**, Isaiah states "*God made and formed the earth; He established it; He created it not void, not empty and not in vain; He formed it to be inhabited*". In **Isaiah 14:12-17,** Isaiah states; "*How art thou (Lucifer) cut down to the ground, You who destroyed the World. For you (Lucifer) said to yourself; "I will ascend into heaven, I will exalt my throne above the stars of Heaven; I will be like the most High". (And) those who see you (Lucifer), will say; - is this the 'one' who made the earth to tremble; - who shook the kingdoms of this world; - who made the world as a wilderness (desolate, empty, void and in a state of confusion)?* This concept is also stated in **Jeremiah 4:23-27**, Jeremiah states "*I beheld the earth, and lo, it was "tohou" (a wilderness, without form, empty, void and in a state of confusion). And the heavens, they had no light. I beheld, and lo, the mountains and hills, they trembled and shook. I beheld, and lo, the fruitful land (hayah) had become (tohou) a wilderness, desolate, empty and void (and in a state of confusion). The cities were crushed by the Lord-God's fierce anger. Then, this is what the Lord-God said; "The whole earth shall lay desolate; yet I, the Lord, will not make a full end or execute complete destruction (of planet earth).* And again in **2nd Peter 3:5-7**, Peter states: "*The people deliberately forgot that - long ago by God's Word, the heavens that were of old and the earth that was of old, were standing out of the water and in the water; by these same waters the (old) world (that prehistoric world) was destroyed; and by this same Word, the present heavens and earth are kept in store, being reserved for destruction by fire on the day of judgment of ungodly people*". **Genesis 1:1-2** state; **"In the beginning - God-created the heavens and the earth. And the earth (hayah) became (tohou) void and without form - a wilderness - desolate and empty; and darkness was upon the face of the deep** *(water)*. **And the Spirit of God (rachaph) moved, viz., was in deep thought".**

In summary, prehistoric "planet" earth was created in stages (generations). Then sometime before Adam and Eve the Lord God made (plant and animal) life beautiful and fruitful. Then, Lucifer was thrown out of Heaven and probably appeared on planet earth with a third of the angels. (Note, these angels then became demon-like and rebellious man like forms that could be part of the fossilized record.) The appearance of Lucifer and his group of demon-like men on planet earth occurred in the very distant past, (way - way) before Adam and Eve were created. The arrival of Lucifer and his band possibly occurred during the Mesozoic Era when dinosaurs and other pre-historic life were so abundant. Then Lucifer rebelled against the Most High (God). This rebellion of Lucifer made the Lord God fiercely angry - so the Lord God partially destroyed his original creation on prehistoric earth.

Note, the Lord God did not execute complete destruction of planet earth. Planet Earth may have physically existed in a desolate, empty, void condition for millions of years while the Lord God (rachaph) moved, or was in deep thought, e.g., hovered over the deep (water). **The Lord God may have been "moved" to create a human being (in His likeness) who could and/or would communicate with Him - willingly.**

Also, during this period of time - the Lord God could have been in deep thought as to how He could or would save His soon to be newly created ones (humans) if they disobeyed or rebelled or sinned against Him. This would have been the time between **Genesis 1:1 and Genesis 1:2** (the "Gap Theory of Creation") before the Lord God began to <u>recreate life</u> as we know it today; **Genesis 1:3-29**.

This lapse in recorded time would have provided ample time for the carbon and hydrogen ions of animal fat (viz., dinosaur fat) to chemically changed (without oxygen) into the carbon - hydrogen molecules of the oil and gas. These oil and gas molecules are now the source of all the oil and gas found so abundant in planet earth's crust - today.

Would it not be interesting to be able to calculate how many dinosaurs were immediately buried (and their fat chemically converted into hydro-carbons without oxygen) in order to form the oil and gas we now use for energy day, by the barrels, for energy!!

THE WORLD THAT WAS BEFORE ADAM!

There was a different planet earth - millions or maybe even billions of years ago. It was different than this present earth age. There were different looking birds, insects, amphibians, fish, reptiles, mammals, plants and possibly even giants with wings (cherubs).

Scientists have divided past earth ages into three ages. These earth ages are: the Paleozoic Age, the Mesozoic Age and Cenozoic Age. The Mesozoic Age is further divided into three periods which are: the Triassic, Jurassic and Cretaceous periods.

It was probably during the Mesozoic Age that Lucifer and the man like forms called cherubs lived on planet earth and actually ruled planet earth. These cherubs may have built cities and lived amongst other prehistoric life.

The **Jurassic period**, which is in the middle of the Mesozoic Age, is known as the period or "age - of – dinosaurs". Scientists have named **the Jurassic period "the age – of – dinosaurs"** because large numbers of various species of dinosaurs lived on planet earth during this period. Fossil evidence indicates - this period was warm and tropical. Fossil evidence also implies that the Jurassic period had a healthy supply of oxygen for the animals to use and carbon dioxide for the plants to thrive. In other words this prehistoric age supported a huge number of species, both plants and animals- though seemingly different from the plants and animals that we see on planet earth today.

_____

Jessie, a boy who lived on planet earth during the twentieth century, was fascinated with prehistoric life, especially the dinosaurs that lived during the Jurassic period of the Mesozoic Era. He often dreamed of living amongst the dinosaurs and riding on their backs.

He read extensively about prehistoric life on pristine (unspoiled by pollution) planet earth. He felt it would be great to tame the dinosaurs and ride on their backs as they roamed over pristine - planet earth.

_____

So, one night Jessie went to bed with a really big wish on his mind. That wish was to visit planet earth during the Mesozoic Era.

And just as soon as Jessie fell asleep, he found himself surrounded by a herd of dinosaurs. It was fantastic.

_____

All of a sudden Bronto, the Brontosauraus, and a large herd of dinosaurs came very close to him.

Jessie recognized all of them and he knew their names. Stego, the Stegosauraus; Allo, the Allosaursus; Tyrano and Rex the Tyrannosaurus brothers; Coelur, the Coelurus; Ptero, the Pterodactyl; Trico, the Triceratops; Anko, the Anklosaurus; Maia, the Maiasaurus; Salta, the Saltasaurus; Cory, the Corythosaurus; Archo the Archaeopteryx; and Campo, the Camptosaurus.

He could hear them talking. They all were excited and talking amongst themselves. They seemed concerned about Lucifer and his band of cherubs. This was because Lucifer was becoming very rebellious, cocky and arrogant. They were wondering what the Most-High was going to do to Lucifer and his band of cherubs.

_____

Stego: "I'm getting very concerned about Lucifer's attitude. He is getting mighty 'cocky' and disrespectful of the Most-High".

_____

Coelur: "I believe you are right Stego. I over-heard Lucifer talking to some of those cherubs. Lucifer told them; "I will ascend into heaven and I will exalt my throne above the stars of the Most-High."

_____

Ptero: (interrupts) "Who is Lucifer?"

_____

Rex: "Lucifer was the Most-High's favorite creation. Of course that was before Lucifer and one third of the cherubs were thrown out of Heaven.

Remember, there was a war in Heaven, and Lucifer lost that war!

That is when the Most-High expelled (threw out of heaven) Lucifer and his band of cherubs. This war in heaven actually took place because of Lucifer's rebellious character. He wanted to usurp the Most High's authority and rule Heaven and Earth." Lucifer and his band of cherubs eventually landed on planet earth thousands of years ago - by my recollection.

_____

Ptero: "Now I know!!! Lucifer is the leader of those cherubs. Even though Lucifer is their leader and handsome, he is not very wise. In fact, Lucifer and his band are the ones that are responsible for building those cities and damming up many of our natural water ways. They have destroyed much of our natural habitat that we have enjoyed for thousands of years. Oh, it actually maybe even millions of years that we have enjoyed this beautiful planet."

Tyrano: "You know, someone should come up a more reliable method of dating those rocks. The Most-High could create with different, smarter beings that walk upright, have a bigger brain and an opposable thumb. This new creation might get it right and not destroy this beautiful earth. This new creation might even protect us and our habitat.

But, for now, those cherubs use the 'uranium to lead' method of dating rocks. Of course, that method of dating rocks makes our planet earth millions or billions of years old. But when they use the 'krypton to argon' method of dating the very same rocks, they get a much younger planet earth.

The 'uranium to lead' method of dating earth rocks is based on the assumed fact; that in the very, very beginning of planet earth, all the rocks contained only uranium and <u>no</u> lead." HOW IGNORANT! HOW UNSCIENTIFIC IS THIS!! _____

Their conversation then drifted back to Lucifer and the other cherubs. _____

Allo: The cherubs that dwell in the nearby cities seem to be in charge of an enclosed energy system. This energy system is very unique - because some periods of light seem to last a very long time and during other periods - the period of light is very short.

Coelur: Well, this might be
because the Most-High has not
yet made a sun to rule the day or a
moon to rule the night. It actually
seems like we live in a warm tropical bubble – right here
on planet earth. _____

Maia: I heard
Lucifer say; "I will
be like the Most-
High, and I will sit
on the mountains
of the assembly in
the side of the
north".

_____

Trico: "Why the north?"

Bronto: (slowly and wisely - answers); "The north is where the Most-High sits. The north represents <u>the Most High's throne</u> and that is why we should do something about this situation on planet earth; before the Most-High gets angry enough to really make some drastic changes on planet earth. These changes might hurt us and might even cause our extinction.

Stego: "What do you think the Most-High will do"? "What kind of changes can the Most-High possibly make"? "We all know there hasn't been any changes on earth, since we were created".

"There is still just one land mass. And those cherubs call it **Pan-gae-a**. It has been surrounded by this large body of water called the **Panthalassa Ocean**. And we have seen those pointed mountains spew out foul, smelling smoke and ashes for years".

––––––––––––––––––––

Trico Jr.: "We've seen the same inland sea's called lakes. Also, for years we have seen the same plants, and birds and all the other living things with which we have shared our resources".

––––––––––––––––

Maia: "Well! I don't believe the Most-High even knows or cares about what is going on down here on planet earth.

_____

Trico: (Asks); "Why do say that?"

you

_____

Anklo: Because, if the Most-High really cared, He would have done something with Lucifer by now".

_____

Campo Jr.: "I fear that the Most-High is just going to get tired of all of Lucifer's activities and shenanigans and really do something horrible. We might even get hurt or even die!"

Coelur: "Now just how could the Most High cause something that horrible? The Most-High would have to literally turn this planet upside down or inside out. And you know that would take a mighty big force."

Allo: "All those steaming mountains could keep on spewing out that foul smelling gas, smoke and hot liquid called lava".

"If that continued, it would darken planet earth and we would not be able to see anything". "That hot stuff called lava could also push all the plants into nearby valleys and cover them up". "This would not only cover up our inland seas and fresh water resources, but that lava would destroy our supply of food and oxygen." "It could also bury us and with **all this fat** that we are made of, **our bodies would turn into oil and gas**". "Just think about that fact because then we would become an important energy source for Lucifer and his band of cherubs". _____

Dimo: "If this happened, I believe planet earth (as we know it) would perish. And planet earth would become desolate, empty and void". "Also, I believe the Most-High would let all those plants set covered up for millions of years". "Then these plants would turn into coal". "Then those cherubs would have another huge source of energy in that new and different earth age."

_____

Campo: "If that hot liquid (they call lava) would fill up all the valleys and inland seas, then the ocean water would rise and flood this entire earth."

Pachy: "We can't live here if all those mountains explode and continue to spew out that terrible foul smelling gas, ashes and hot liquid."

Salta Sr.: "I'm just not going to be concerned about any of this stuff." "I will just choose to believe – 'life will go on as it has for millions and/or billions of years'."

————————

Allo: "No! No! We all need to go to the city to talk to Lucifer; we need to plead with him to be more content with ruling his kingdom here on planet earth". "I think that planet earth is beautiful and perfect just the way it is". "In fact, you all know that we truly live in a warm, tropical, greenhouse bubble". The temperature remains tropical year after year. That is the reason we have all these lushes green tropical plants to eat.

————————

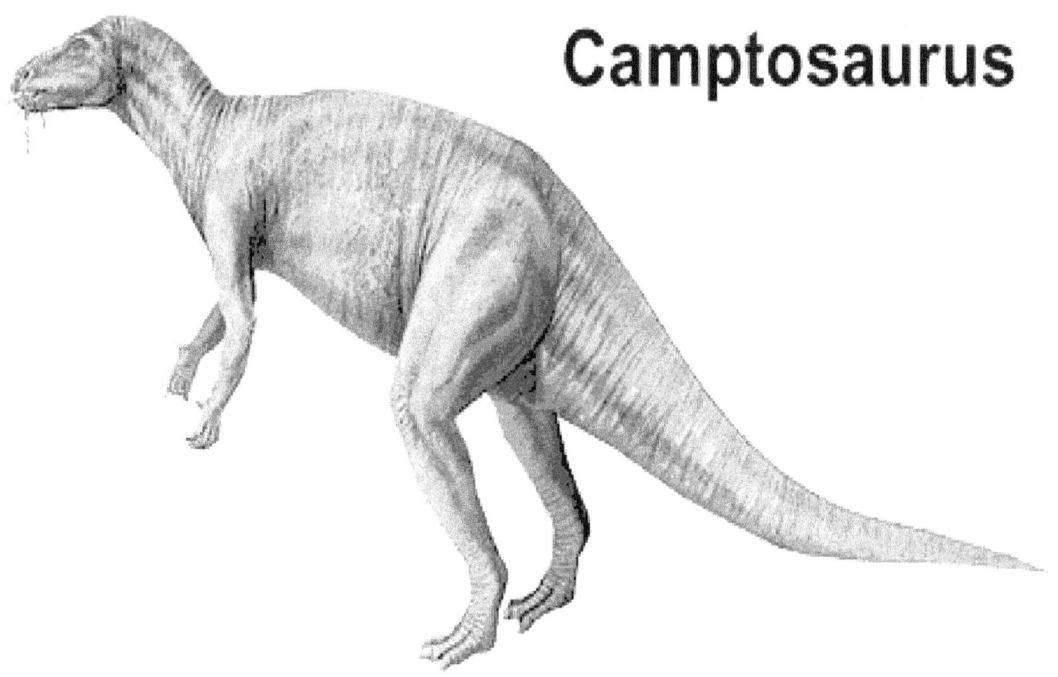

Camptosaurus

Campo #2: "I think one of those meteors from outer space could come crashing down and knock planet earth into a different orbit. If this occurred, the temperature would certainly get so cold that snow and ice would collect to form glaciers again. Either way, we would not survive and all of us would become extinct."

———————————

Bronto: "Yes we need to talk with Lucifer, because I know we can't live here long if it freezes". "I like living here just the way it is - right now".

"However, I do believe it was very cold in the past and that there was an ice age before we were created". "That is because I see evidence of glacier activity all around". "That era must have been really cold". "And I don't even want to think about what would happen to me if it were to freeze again."

_____

Archo: "Lucifer is the Most-High's favorite creation and He's not going to let anything "bad"

happen to Lucifer or those other cherubs. Look how beautiful they all are - especially Lucifer.

_____

Dyno: "Well I know one thing for sure; if the Most-High does something and all these life forms including become extinct, the Most High could start over and make a new earth with new or different kinds of living things, both plants and animals.

us

In fact, His new creation may be smarter than we are.

————————————

All of a sudden Jessie heard a very loud explosion in the distance; and felt the mountains shake and saw lava spew out of thousands of cone shaped mountains. There was a very huge amount of ash and hot liquid that began rolling down the mountain side. It was pushing all the prehistoric vegetation and prehistoric animals, even the huge dinosaurs, into the existing valleys and inland lakes.

All of the pre-historic plants and animals were covered immediately with this large flow of lava.

Then Jessie awoke from his dream and began to think. He surmised that huge numbers of "fatty" prehistoric animals, viz., the dinosaurs, were pushed into the inland seas and valleys. And because these animals were covered immediately without a source of oxygen to decompose their bodies into water vapor and carbon dioxide, the fat in the dinosaur's body would turn in oil and gas in this "anaerobic environment.

Jessie knew that fat mostly contained hydrogen atoms and carbon atoms and that without oxygen these elements would form hydrocarbons. All of the fat from prehistoric

animals would begin forming the large oil and gas deposits that have been discovered beneath earth's surface today.

Then Jessie began to calculate how many dinosaurs it would take to fill up their car's gas tank.

_____

Now, we find the Most-High is hovering over the deep (water) of planet earth. The Most High is brooding, viz., meditating and in deep thought about recreating planet earth.

Wow! Look what the Most-High had on his mind?

_____

Dinosaur Facts

Camptosaurus, 20 ft (6 m) long, from Europe and North America

Aliosaurus, 39 ft (12 m) long, from North America

Stegosaurus, 30 ft (9 m) long, from North America

Coelurus, 7 ft (2 m) long, from North America

Saltasaurus

Tyrannosaurus

Triceratops

Corythosaurus

Pachycephalosaurus

Euoplocephalus

DINOSAUR FACTS

#1: What is a Dinosaur? When scientists talk of dinosaurs, they mean **a unique kind of creature that lived on land during the Triassic, Jurassic, or Cretaceous period**.

#2: What are the **Ages of Dinosaurs**? They are **Triassic, Jurassic and Cretaceous periods.**

#3: **The Smartest Dinosaur was; The Troodon**! Scientists measure smartness by figuring out how big an animal compared to its body. This is called "encephalization quotient." Troodon wins! Even so, they think he was only about as smart as a modern possum.

#4: **The Dumbest Dinosaur was;. The stegosaurus**! It had a brain as big as a walnut in a body weighing nearly two tons! A nicer way to say this is: Stegosaurus was"less smart" than a Troodon!

#5: **The Fastest Dinosaur was; Coelophysis and other Ornithomimosaurs**. Scientists think these dinosaurs ran up to 30 miles per hour for short distances!

#6: **The Biggest Dinosaurs were Saurpods**. Seismosaurus was 165 feet long with tail. Arentinosaurus was the heaviest at 100 tons. The Brachiosaurus was 39 feet high (which helped it reach branches in trees). Giganotosaurus was the largest hunting dinosaur, at 46 feet long and up to 8 tons!

#7: The Smallest Dinosaur was the Saltopus. It was only 3 feet long, and weighed about five pounds.

#8: **What Killed the Dinosaurs**? No one really knows! Scientists have several theories:

    Meteor hits the earth!
    Lots of volcanic eruptions!
    Climate Changes (over a long period of time)

#9: Dinosaurs Lived on Land! Many prehistoric sea creatures lived at the same time as dinosaurs. However, they were not true dinosaurs! **Kronosaurus was believed to be the largest of all the sea reptiles.** It grew to be almost 42 feet long.

#10: **Dinosaurs First Appeared; in the Triassic period, around 200 million years ago.** A group of reptiles from the late Permian Period (archosaurs) became the best hunters on land. They developed special features in their skulls and how they walked (having an upright body with their legs under their body), which made them dinosaurs.

#11: What do Dinosaur eggs look like? **Dinosaur eggs have many shapes and sizes**. Some eggs have been documented to be 16" long or more. The first dinosaur egg fossils were found in France in 1869. Many dinosaur eggs found still have their original shells.

Fossil Fuels (Crude Oil, Natural Gas and Coal) were once alive!

Fossil fuels (crude oil and natural gas), were once alive! They were formed from prehistoric plants and animals that lived possibly millions of years ago; way - way - before man, as we know man with 46 chromosomes, was created.

Can you imagine what the planet earth must have looked like millions of years or so ago? The land mass we live on today was just being formed. Probably there were swamps, bogs and seas everywhere. The climate was probably warmer and ancient trees and plants grew both in the water and on dry land. Tiny one-celled organisms called phyto-plankton floated in the ocean and fern-like plants grew both in the water and on the earth's surface. Also, there were many huge magnificent prehistoric animals. Fossils indicate strange looking animals walked on the land, and just as weird looking animals swam in the rivers and seas.

When huge numbers of these ancient (prehistoric) animals died and became buried in an "anaerobic environment" (i.e., an environment without the presence of oxygen) under layers and layers of mud, rock, and sand they decomposed into hydrocarbons. Eventually, and maybe suddenly, hundreds and sometimes thousands of feet of earth covered these once living, fat containing - creatures that represented prehistoric life.

Note, Prehistoric life refers to life that existed on planet earth before man as we know man -existed; that is before humans were created with 46 chromosomes and a genetic code like what we have today. This genetic code, for example, has genes for eye color located on the same chromosome and at the same gene loci (address). If there was another animal with 46 chromosome but their genes for eye color were on different chromosomes and at different gene loci then that creature would not contain the human genome.

During the millions of years (eras) that may have come and gone, these dead plants and animals slowly decomposed in an "anaerobic environment" and formed the fossil fuels that we use today for energy. Different types of fossil fuels are formed depending on the combination of animal and/or plant debris that was also buried at that time. The composition of these types of fossil fuels also depended on how long that material was buried, and on what conditions of temperature and pressure existed after they were buried and when they were decomposing in that anaerobic environment.

For example, oil and natural gas were created from organisms that lived and/or died in a water environment and were buried under layers of ocean or land sediments. Long after the great prehistoric seas and rivers vanished or dried-up, heat, pressure and bacteria combined to compress the organic material under layers of silt. In most areas, a thick liquid called crude oil formed first, but in deeper, hotter regions underground, the heating process continued until natural gas was formed. Over time, some of this oil and natural gas began working its way upward through the earth's crust until they ran into rock formations called "cap-rocks" that are dense enough to prevent these liquid fossil fuels from seeping to the surface. It is from under these "cap-rocks" that most oil and natural gas is extracted today.

Similar types of forces created coal, however the biggest difference is - Coal formed from the dead remains of vegetation (i.e., trees, ferns and other plants) that thrived during the pre-historic eras. In some areas, such as portions of what-is-now the eastern United States, coal was formed when swamp vegetation was covered by sea water. Sea water, back then, must have contained a large amount of sulfur; and as silt eventually covered the various types of prehistoric vegetation and the seas dried up, the sulfur was left behind in the coal, usually under silt or sand-stone rock.

Today, as part of the coal mining process, scientists are busy working on ways to take the sulfur out of coal. This is because when coal containing sulfur - burns, the sulfur can become an air pollutant - forming sulfuric acid. Some coal deposits, however, were formed from freshwater swamps which had ery little sulfur in them. These coal deposits are located largely in the western part of the United States and this coal does not have sulfur in them or if it does, it is very little.

Note: It takes 200 feet of plant (vegetative) material (i.e., leaves and wood) to make 40 feet of coal.

OIL

Oil is basically any neutral, non-polar, hydrogen-carbon containing chemical substance that is a viscous (thick) liquid at present biotic temperatures. It is immiscible (does not mix) with water but is soluble in alcohols or ethers. Oils have a higher than gas concentration of hydrogen and carbon and are usually slippery to touch. They are also very flammable. The origin of oils may be either animal or vegetable, and may be volatile or non-volatile.

Note; volatile refers to the fact these organic chemicals can evaporate rapidly in the form of vapor and non-volatile means that these organic chemicals do not evaporate or vaporize readily.

Types of Oils: (Mineral oils and Organic oils)

Mineral oils refer to crude oil, or petroleum, and its refined components are collectively known as petrochemicals. Petrochemicals or crude oils are crucial resources in our modern economy.

Crude oil originates from ancient fossilized organic materials, such as zooplankton, algae, whales, fish as well as land animals such as dinosaurs and other "fat" containing animals or plants that died in large numbers and were buried immediately in an "anaerobic environment" (an environment that contains no oxygen) usually in ancient seas. Then, over many years, the "geochemical processes", viz., heat and pressure, converted the hydrogen and carbon ions of fat into were converted (viz., changed chemically) into oil which is also known as hydrocarbons.

The name, mineral oil, is a misnomer in that minerals are not the source of mineral oil;- ancient plants and animals are the source of mineral oils, i.e., crude oils! Minerals are technically not organic. Mineral oil is organic. However, crude oil is classified as a "mineral oil" instead of as an "organic oil" because its organic origin was very remote at the time of crude oils discovery.

Note; most mineral oils, viz., crude oils are obtained in the vicinity of rocks, underground traps, and sands.

Note also, organic oils are more correctly known as cooking oils; they are technically not minerals oils. These organic oils are associated with present or living animal or plant life and therefore they are usually "edible" oils. Organic oils are produced by remarkably diverse groups of plants, animals, and other organisms through natural metabolic processes.

Lipid is a type of organic oil; however, it is not directly used for cooking. It is the scientific term for fatty acids, triglycerides, steroids and similar chemicals often found in the organic oils produced by living things. Organic oils may also contain other edible chemicals such as proteins, waxes and alkaloids.

Both mineral oils/crude oils and edible organic oils have a high concentration of hydrogen and carbon and they do not contain oxygen or are considerably lacking in oxygen compared to other organic compounds.

Applications of oils

Cosmetics: Oils are applied to hair to give it a lustrous look, to prevent tangles and roughness as well as to stabilize the hair and promote hair growth.

Religion: Oils are commonly used in ritual anointments. As a particular example, holy anointing oil has been an important ritual liquid for both Judaism and Christianity healing.

Painting: Color pigments are easily suspended in oil, making it suitable as a supporting medium for paints. The oldest known existing oil paintings date back to 650 AD.

Heat transfer: Oils are used as coolants in oil cooling, for instance in electric transformers. Oils are also used to enhance heating in other applications, such as cooking (especially in frying).

Lubrication: Oils are commonly used as lubricants. Mineral oils are more commonly used as machine lubricants than biological "organic" oils are. Whale oil is preferred for lubricating clocks, because it does not evaporate and does not collect dust. However, its use was banned in 1980. As no suitable substitute for whale oil is available, it is still used in space science but in very small quantities.

Note: In the 18th and 19th centuries, whale oil was commonly used for lamps. However, whale oil was replaced with natural gas and then electricity.

Note also, not all oils used as fuel are mineral oils/crude oils. One example is corn which is now being used to make biodiesel and vegetable oil fuel.

Fuel Oil: Some oils burn in liquid or aerosol form, generating light and heat which can be used directly or converted into other forms of energy such as electricity or mechanical work. To obtain fuel oil, crude oil is pumped from the ground and then shipped via oil tankers to oil refineries. At the refinery, the **crude oil is converted** into **diesel fuel** (petro-diesel), alkanes (**ethane, propane**, etc.), **fuel oil** (the heaviest of commercial fuels), **kerosene, benzene, gasoline** (petro), as well as **jet fuel**and **liquefied petroleum gas.** Note: Alkanes (ethane, propane) consist only of hydrogen and carbon atoms in which all bonds are single bonds and the carbon atoms are not joined in cyclic structures but instead form an open chain.

Note also; A 42 gallon barrel (U.S.) of crude oil produces approximately 10 gallons of diesel, 4 gallons of jet fuel, 19 gallons of gasoline, 7 gallons of other products, 3 gallons split between heavy fuel oil nd liquefied petroleum gases, and 2 gallons of heating oil.

Crude Oil and its Chemical Structure

The smallest unit of a substance, which still retains the characteristics of that substance, is called a molecule. Molecules can only be divided into atoms. Atoms are different elements. For example, all molecules of water are identical and have the characteristics of water. The two atoms of hydrogen
and the one atom of oxygen (H_2O) is a molecule of water. Neither hydrogen or carbon atoms on their own have any of the characteristics of water.

Crude oils are <u>mixtures</u> of many different molecules and they are often difficult to separate. However, crude oils can be separated during the refining process to yield the various petroleum products such as: gasoline, kerosene propane, fuel oil, lubricating oil, wax, and asphalt. These substances mainly consist of compounds that have only two elements: hydrogen (H) and carbon (C). Therefore, they
are called "**hydrocarbons**".

Refining crude oil involves two kinds of processes to produce the products that are so essential for energy in our modern society. First, there are physical processes which simply refine (separate) the crude oil (without altering its molecular structure) into useful products such as lubricating oil or fuel oil. Second, there are chemical or other processes which alter the molecular structure and produce a wide range of products such as cosmetics, oil base paints, etc., and most of them are known by the general term **petrochemicals**.

Crude oil can be refined into a wide variety of hydro-carbons/petrochemicals. Petrochemicals are the refined components of crude oil and the chemical products made from them. Petrochemicals are used as detergents, fertilizers, medicines, cosmetics, paints, plastics, synthetic fibers, and synthetic rubber.

Hydrocarbons are petrochemicals and petrochemicals are hydrocarbons. Hydrocarbons may be gaseous, liquid, or solid at normal temperature and pressure, depending on the number and arrangement of the carbon atoms in their molecules. At present day bio-temperatures, those hydro-carbon molecules with up to 4 carbon atoms are gaseous; those with 20 or more are solid; those in between are liquid. Crude oils are liquid but may contain gaseous or solid compounds (or both) in solution. Heavy crude oil is usually a liquid at room temperature, however, as the temperature cools and the number of carbon atoms each molecule increases, the closer it is to being a semi-solid or solid (i.e. the more carbon atoms its molecules contain make this hydrocarbon more likely to become a solid at cool temperatures). Light crude oils (those that contain only a few carbon atoms) will remain liquid even at very low temperatures.

The simplest hydrocarbon is methane, a gas consisting of one carbon atom and four hydrogen atoms. Propane is a straight chain molecule with 3 carbon and 8 hydrogen atoms. Iso-butane is a branched chain molecule consisting of 4 carbon and 10 hydrogen atoms. More complex molecules occur when one or more hydrogen atoms are replaced by hydrocarbon groups or by the condensing or "stacking" of one or more rings. A simple example of this occurs in naphthalene (C_{10}, H_8).

As the molecular structure of naphthalene becomes characterized by denser carbon atoms and even further stacking, we enter the realm of "heavy oils". One of the most complex examples of "stacking" occurs in asphaltenes. Asphaltenes are distillation products from oil refineries that are used as asphalt on roads.

Thus, you can see that the number of hydrogen atoms associated with a given skeleton of carbon atoms may vary. When the chain or ring carries the full complement of hydrogen atoms, the hydrocarbon is said to be "saturated". When less than the full complement of hydrogen atoms is present in a hydrocarbon chain or ring, the hydrocarbon is said to be "unsaturated". These terms apply to both mineral oils and edible "organic" oils.

All fossil fuels have played and still play important roles in providing the energy that every man, woman, and child in the United States uses every-day in today's world. With better technology for finding and using fossil fuels, each can play an equally important role in the future.

References: King James Bible

2nd Peter 3:5-7; (5) Where-by the world that then was, being overflowed with water - perished. But the heavens and the earth, which are now, by the same Word of God are kept in store, reserved unto fire against the day of judgment.

Isaiah 14:12-17; (12) How are thou fallen from heaven, O Lucifer, son of the morning; For thou has said in thine heart, "I will ascend into heaven, I will exalt my throne above the stars of God; I will sit also upon the mount of the congregation, in the sides of the north; I will ascend above the heights of the clouds; I will be like the most high."

You shall be brought down to Sheol, to the lowest depths of the pit. Those who see you will gaze at you, and consider you, saying; "is this the one who made the earth tremble, who shook kingdoms; Who made the world (**tohou**) as a wilderness and destroyed its cities, who did not open the house of his prisoners?

Jeremiah 4:23-27; (23) "I beheld the earth, and indeed it (**hayah**) was made to become without form and void; and the heavens, they had no light. I beheld the mountains, and indeed they trembled, and all the hills moved back and forth. I beheld and indeed there was no man, and all the birds of the heavens had fled. I beheld, and indeed the fruitful land (hayah) became (tohou) void, a wilderness, desolate and empty". (27) For thus says the Lord; "The whole land shall be desolate; yet I will not make a full end."

Genesis 1:2; (2) And the earth (hayah) became (tohou) void and without form; and darkness was upon the face of the deep. And the spirit of God moved (brooded) upon the face of the waters.

Genesis 2:4-5; (4) This is the generations (ages) of the heavens and the earth when they were created in the day that the Lord God made earth and heaven. (5) Now no shrub of the field was yet in the earth and no plant of the field had yet sprouted, (and every plant of the field before it was in the earth and every herb of the field before it grew for the Lord God had not sent rain upon the earth and there was no man to cultivate the ground.

Isaiah 45:18; (18) for thus saith the Lord - that created the heavens and formed the earth. He hath established it. He created it not (tohou) desolate, empty, void or in vain.

Hebrew Definitions used in this text:
  Hayah; was sometimes interpreted to be "was" but meant "became or to become".
  Tohou; can mean any of the following; void, without form, empty, vain, or wilderness.
  Rachaph; was interpreted "moved" but meant "brooded or in deep thought".

Note: Lucifer is another name for Satan or morning star. He took 1/3 of the angels out of heaven thousands or millions of years before Adam and Eve were created. He descended to earth sometime in the dateless past (prehistoric). He then tried to ascend back into heaven and take over God's throne. It was this rebellion against God's authority that made God angry enough to destroy His original creation on planet earth - that is referenced in 2nd Peter 3:5-7 as perished.

Denise Sharbono Marks, M.D. - Biography

Denise is now a retired medical doctor who has renewed her interest in writing. She specializes in writing about subjects related to science, religion, medicine, nutrition, and safe and effective means of weight loss.

Born in Billings, Montana, Denise graduated in 1965 from the Huntley Project High School in Worden, Montana. She then joined the U.S. Marine Corps and served from 1965 - 1968. After finishing her military obligation she used the GI Bill to obtain a college education. She received her BS degree in Health and Physical Education with a minor in Biology and a major in Chemistry. She began teaching Chemistry, Biology and General Science as well as Health and Physical Education in Rayville, Louisiana between 1971 and 1982. After one of her chemistry students got accepted into Medical School, she realized she also could learn to become a medical doctor.

Denise received her M.D. degree in 1986 from Louisiana State University Medical Center in Shreveport, La. In 1988, she received her Arkansas medical license and then moved to Arkansas where she began her medical practice in rural Arkansas.

Denise is the proud and happy mother of 2 adult sons and a grandmother. In fact, she is dedicating this book to her two sons, Jason and Justin Sharbono, who had to sacrifice their time with her while she studied to become a medical doctor. Denise is a member of Twin Lakes Marine and the Marine Corps League. As a veteran of the Vietnam era she continues to help veterans, especially with post traumatic issues and depression, overcome some of the issues that hinder them from achieving a better quality of life through diet, counseling and medication.

Her mission still remains "to serve others" by teaching or instructing them on how they can become a healthier individual by using natural (food) nutrients as well as teaching those who are interested in a Biblical explanation of the origins of life and the universe.

Denise enjoyed putting puzzles together with her family during the cold, wintery days in Montana. She was also interested in getting to the truth behind any scientific theory even when that theory was presented as fact. She believes the Bible is the infallible word of God, and can be profitable for not only doctrine, but also for edification (intellectual, moral, or spiritual improvement), reproof (correct gently) and instruction (knowledge or information to be imparted). She has spent many hours studying the scriptures, especially those verses that gave her a plausible answer as to "why the rocks and the fossils found in them may be millions of years old and yet man as we know man is only about 6,000 years old (5,775 by Jewish history in 2014 AD). Note, this human being that was created had the ability to write about history and this written history is only about 6,000 years old. This figure, 6,000 years (5,775 BC), goes along with the genealogy found in both the Old and New Testament of the Bible. Her latest book, "**The World That Was - Before Adam**" is the result of this research.

www.ingramcontent.com/pod-product-compliance
Lightning Source LLC
Chambersburg PA
CBHW081125280526
45787CB00007B/2985